THE SHARK IN THE PARK

Mark Watson

for Vito & Julia

This book is dedicated to Isabel Polo, Andrew Hirst and Laura Basso
Illustrations by Pablo Michau.

The air is misty, bright and cool,
the morning Michael walks to school.

At the boundary of the park he waits,
nervously he hesitates.

The day warms up, the sun shines down
and Mike walks on, into town.

Gnarly branches, crook and tight,
curl around the ghostly light.

Suddenly he freezes, weak at the knees,
what is that swimming beneath the trees?

There's a shark in the park! How can this be?
These terrible beasts live in the sea.

Blue above, white beneath,
the blackest eyes, the sharpest teeth.

Its fin is huge, a towering dorsal.
Mike feels small, a tiny morsel.

Although he can't believe his eyes,
he needs to move to stay alive.

Through the grassy surf his feet pound,
he runs into a small playground.

No time to breathe, no time to shout,
he jumps onto the roundabout.

It rolls and sways with a dizzy motion,
as though a boat upon the ocean.

Crash! Smash! From beneath,
the shark explodes, fins and teeth.

Into the air his schoolbag soars,
it's ripped to shreds by might jaws.

The bus is there, he won't be beaten,
he's faster now, his homework eaten.

He sees a sight he can't believe,
the bus pulls out and starts to leave.

Just before the bus is gone,
Mike shouts "STOP" and stumbles on.

Deprived now of a tasty bite,
the shark sinks slowly out of sight.

Day after day and all through the week,
Mike battles the shark with a different technique.

He's still awake in darkest night,
his mum has long turned off the light.

With his dad's helmet and fishing pole,
Mike decides to risk it all.

The line goes tight and without a sound,
he reels the shark OUT OF THE GROUND!

Before it can consume him whole...

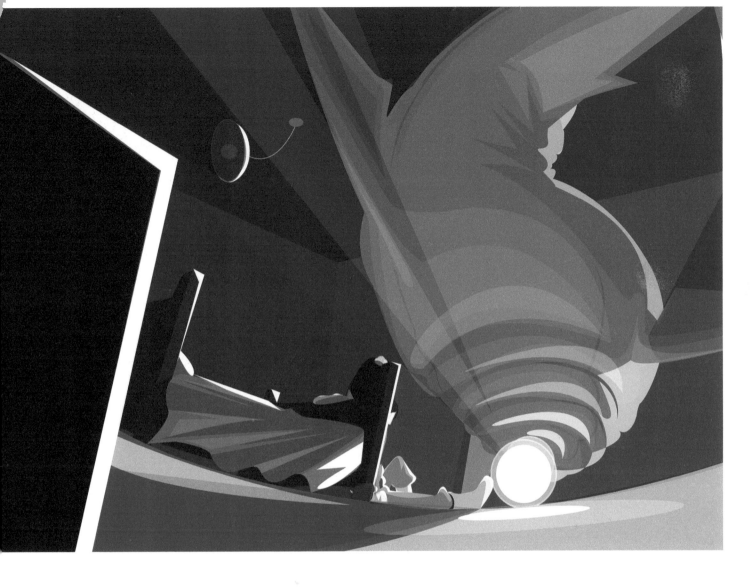

...it's sucked into the goldfish bowl.

Now here he is, the fearsome beast,
fat, content and tame.
Bobbing around on the mantelpiece,
between some books and a picture frame.

THE
END

There are more brilliant picture books by Mark Watson for you to collect:

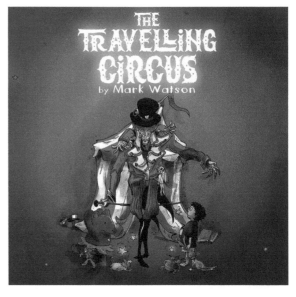

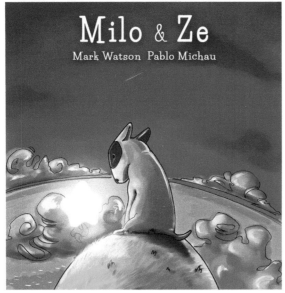

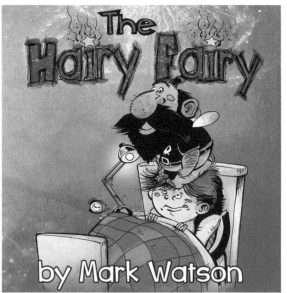

And visit www.markwatsonchildrensbooks.com for

all the latest book news, activities and fun.

CPSIA information can be obtained
at www.ICGtesting.com
Printed in the USA
LVHW072010101218
599929LV00002B/35/P